00:00:00

The Timeless Whispers

Yoshita Gurnani

BookLeaf Publishing

India | USA | UK

Dedicated:

*1. To my family, my husband, my daughters and
my fellow travellers on the journey of
self-discovery.*

*2. To the beauty of those empty moments and the
sense of fullness it brings!*

*3. Lastly and profoundly to my parents – Father
Mother, I am, because YOU are.*

Acknowledgement

I am forever grateful to:

My loved ones– my mother, my husband and my daughters, who endured odd hours of writing sessions and early-morning musings. With all the love and patience, they gave me profound and powerful listening.
My close soulful friends and siblings, who agreed to test run these poems on them.

My writing mentors, who believed in me.

The BookLeaf Publishing team, who introduced me to a platform.

I am also indebted to the poets and authors who have inspired me to find my voice.

And to the timeless moments of stillness and chaos that shaped my perspective.

Thank you for being part of this journey.

May these words of whispers find a home in your heart.

Preface

Where the line between serenity and chaos blur,

I find myself lost and found,

Where I hear a whispered silence,

Where stillness is both calming and unsettling,

I wonder where I belong.

In this collection of poems, '00:00:00' – The Timeless Whispers,

I invite you to join me on my journey of unrevealed and unspoken moments.

Through the quiet hours of 'now' and the moments of travelling back, I have sought out a few whispered silences in the midst of a chaos where the time refused to move and stood still with me, to let me whisper my moments that were revealed to me in my quiet and not so quiet inward journey.

I hope with the simplicity and authenticity of my thoughts may relate to you profoundly. You will experience being recreated as the whispers from the pages shall spark a change in your perspective.

I am nothing but you, and you have created me and I am recreating you.

May these Rhapsodies leave you with a sense of belonging in the blur and leave you with love and love only. I asked 3 questions to myself and got my answers, and here I share:

1. What do I want the readers to take away from this book?

I want the readers to:
– Reflect on the timeless moments that shape our lives.
– Find solace in shared human experiences.
– Explore their own emotions, thoughts and desires.
– Appreciate the depth and the beauty of poetry that has the power to transform.
– Feel inspired, comforted or challenged to new perspectives

2. How do I want my poetry to resonate with others?

I envision my poetry:

– Resonating emotionally, evoking empathy, simplicity and connection.

– Sparking introspection, sparking transformation, self-reflection and personal growth.

– Promising comfort, courage or guidance during challenging times.

– Inspiring creativity, imagination or new ideas.

– Fostering a sense of community and shared understanding.

3. What unique perspective do I bring to the literary landscape?

– My personal experiences, personal interactions, my background, my worldview.

– Exploring authenticity, vulnerability and universal love.

– Creating and blending styles, forms or genres in my own innovative ways.

– Offering authenticity, simplicity in the expression.

– Sharing insights gained from my own struggles, triumphs or transformations.

Mission Statement :

With '00:00:00 – The Timeless Whispers', I aim to craft a transformative and introspective collection of poems that captures the essence of the human experience.

By sharing my unique perspective and voice, I strive to:

– Create a sanctuary for self-discovery and contemplation.

– Stimulate empathy, understanding and community.

– Leave a reviving, lasting impression in the hearts and minds of readers.

May 'oo:oo:oo – The Timeless Whispers' become a beacon for those seeking transformation, inspiration, an opening and insight, reminding us that in the stillness of the timeless moments, our truest selves are revealed.

It's a journey to self-discovery and nourishing connection through poetry.

1. Who am I

Who am I

Sometimes I wonder,
Who am I

Am I my name or personality,
Someone's daughter or identity,
Maybe I am a mother or a wife,
A sister, a friend or am I just life.

What makes me, what designs me,
What constitutes me, what am I.

Am I my emotion or just a thought,
Am I a fleeting dream or a moment caught,
Am I a celebrated fest or those tiny little
steps,
Am I an illusion or just compromises at rest.

Am I my doubts or the suppressed fear,
Am I the reflection of my near and dear.

Am I a bounce after a falling fall,
Or maybe the failing, while I crawl,
Am I a medium to the living lives,
That I live with, to just not survive.

Am I gold, bold stroke of fate,
Or just the great blend of traits,
I may be a mixture of one and all,
All the people living or on the wall.

A woman I am,
Made from the little pieces of you,
Made from little whispers and little vibrant
hues,
Produced from living unions that jam,
It's only love and love that I am.

2. Keep a little of me

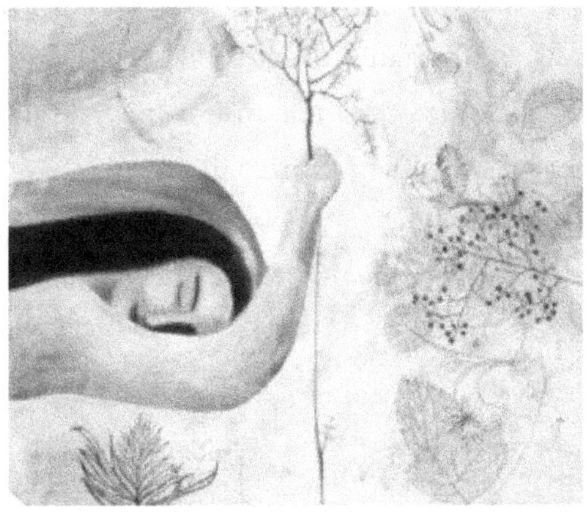

Keep a little of me

Because I am made for thee
But you can keep a little of me.

In the depths of your soul, I'll reside
A little piece of my heart always inside

Though we may part, I'll stay with you
That fragment of my part, forever true

When your eyes shine, it's me with you
Our love divine will always reflect you

Because I am made for thee
But you can keep a little of me and I'll be free
And I will love you more, till eternity.

3. Reveal

Reveal

When you arrive,
why fear breaks in.

She in her silk nightgown,
why feels nude in.

Her soft, subtle blush skin,
Why lost its colour as though, rubbed in.

The sweet curve on her face,
Now appears inverted and fades in.

Sounds of her past laughter,
Are now songs of cries for him.

Why do you hurry,
Things for her are now settling in.

You bring the sounds of silence,
Deafening her ears, and nothing seeps in.

You leave her frozen,
While the sunshine moves in.

Ohh, she is numb and no tears,
Waiting for her heart yet to beat in.

Oh Death,
Come like a gentle breeze,
Make her feel that life is singing.

Whisper soft to her soul,
As she is still grappling from her core in.

So please come and reveal the truth,
That you are not the end but a new
beginning.

4. I will live as a Tree

I will live as a Tree

Here you all have finally come
To see I am gone or simply numb.

When I die, just simply do not cry
Let me leave in silence and tears dry.

Use red cotton cloth after I lay on wooden
bars
My body dipped in fragrant, fresh flowers.

Don't elaborate the cremation display
The people's gossip and stories at play.

Do not leave me on an electric tray
I would love to rest on the woods I lay.

When I have turned with fire to ashes grey
Hold me softly as I am ready to go happy and
gay.

Don't let me dip and simply flow
My particles tiny would love to again grow.

Add me to the soil from where I came
I will live as a tree in a far-fetched plain.

5. Romancing with Life

Romancing with Life

When I am alone, I try tonic in gin,
Although I know it's an unknown spin.

The roads will always travel far and far,
My journey is bound to have a little scar.

New paths unfold and doubts may arise,
Why do I tremble with my anxious eyes.

Isn't my each new breath a fresh design,
The only thing that stays is the breath of
mine.

The present always feels like slipping away,
Yet I cling to what's next with each breath
sway.

I wait for joy in some future zone,
So insane, not aware that nothing's my own.

I think I will be happy and joyful,
When accomplishments pile or success is full.

A promotion, a hit or Oscars 's gleam,
But isn't joy 'now' in this fleeting dream?

In the moment's beauty, I find my pace,
Not in some tomorrow, my heart's race.

For time keeps moving and moments decay,
Leaving me with now, to seize the day.

Let go of fears and embrace the new,
Finding joy in the journey even if no clue.

To be living in the present is as free,
Romancing with Life, wild as be!!

6. I am Home

I am Home

When I am with myself, I am home,
In the depths of my soul, I am never alone.
A power resides, a truth reveals,
The courage to be me and my heart's
concealed.

When the world outside is dark and cold,
And the voices of doubt begin to unfold,
I remember that my worth is not defined,
By the noise of others, but the fire that burns
refined.

Let it rage, let it roar, let it guide me through,
For in its warmth, I will find the strength to
break through.

In solitude, the inner strength takes hold,
My compassion and vulnerability unfolds,
I no longer am bound to stories external,
I will know it's me, me the story eternal.

I may wander, lost and far from my core,
Yearning to return, to find my heart's score.
The answer lies within, a truth to embrace,
Home is not just a place but a sense of inner
grace.

I journey inward and claim my rightful place,
Where love and acceptance fill up my face.
For when I am with myself, I am home,
Nothing stops me, however, I am yet to be
known.

7. The Train is Leaving

The train is leaving

In June 1994, when I was twenty-four,
A mother of two with love galore.
My two little girls, so pretty and sweet,
One 4 years and the other 4 months to meet.

I boarded a train with the fear in my gut,
Alone with my babies, my heart's in a rut.
The train sped on through rain and night,
I held my little ones so close and tight.

At a station stop, I rushed out to fetch,
Milk for my baby, and my heart's a stretch.
I pleaded a man to fill the bottle fast,
As I watched the train, my heart aghast.

In the crowded shop, I pushed and prayed,
I rushed to get back on the train, was delayed.
A shouting man warned, 'Your train is
leaving'!
I dropped the bottles, my heart stopped
beating.

I ran wilder, faster than the train,
To catch my cabin, my heart's in pain.
A hand reached out from the crowded train
door,
I grabbed it tight as people pushed me once
more.

Tears flowed free as I held my girls close,
Fear and heartbeat in a frantic propose.
This wasn't just the end, also a dream
repeated,
A series of nightmares, my heart perpetually
seated.

Even now I relive that desperate dash,
A mother's fear forever etched in my flash.
No escape from the memory, no respite,
A chain of dreams and my heart forever in
flight.

And still, I wonder, did I make it in time?
The fear of missing the train still haunts my
mind.
A memory that stays a lingering fear,
That moment had changed me forever, dear.

8. Rising by Falling

Rising by Falling
What it would be to fall in love with you.

A union so divine it fills the space,
I am rising in love when you embrace.
It leaves tears in my eyes,
While my little soul smiles,
When I love and long for you,
Am Rising, by falling in love with you.

A longing so deep,
It transcends all sound,
I am free and unbound,
With no self to be found,
In this love, am I lost in you,
Am Rising, by falling in love with you.

I wonder how it would be
To be one with you
When there is no more of me and you,
There is no me and no I,
Just a reflection of YOU,
Am Rising, falling in love with you.

Longing for you is nothing,
But an ultimate chance,
That has no boundaries enhanced,
This life has no meaning,
But only one dance with you,
Am Rising, falling in love with you.

9. Dark Night

Dark night

I wonder how darkness,
Brings its dark delight,
Gathering sounds and tones,
In black and grey light.
In the woods when darkness,
Plays and dances by,
The secrets take birth,
And the fears are born to sigh.

Courage stays,
While sounds sing to secret tunes,
'Will' keeps you going,
Through all the threat-filled dunes.
In the night all that happens,
That day would never dare,
Slipping into the hands of the unknown,
Dark and unfair.

When the only saviour is hope,
And the trust, your only scope,
You navigate the dark with a heart,
That loves and still solely copes.

10. Free fall

Free fall

'Hushed whispers of fate, as the car plunges deep,
Nooraa, cradled by waters, in a dark jungle's keep'.

Some falls are meant to lift us high,
When our efforts fade, the universe replies.

We feel we've lost all and left everything behind,
But remember, ahead lies a destination, undefined.

And, as we sail through the unknown tides,
While tears may fall, our soul silently prays inside.

With all futures revealed, what surprise awaits?
When our story unfolds, life smiles and fate creates.

A new path emerges like a sunrise after a very dark night,
Guiding us forward with flow so gentle and there's no fight.

11. Sunkissed

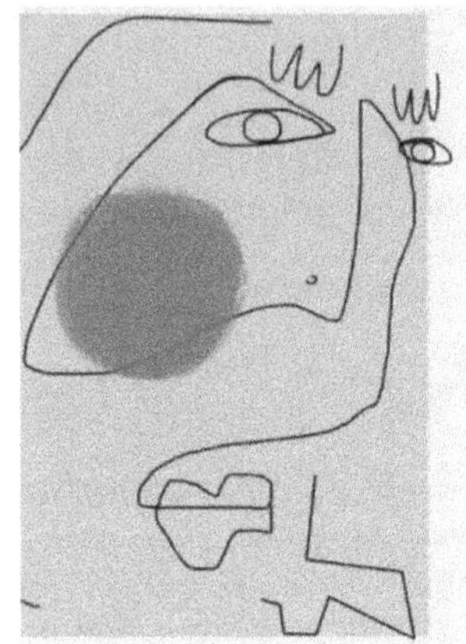

Sunkissed

What is a relationship but a test of wills?
A bond between two souls or a fragile thrill?
Do we enter to lift each other high?
Or to pull down and watch the other cry?

Respect is broken; the heart is shattered too,
The pieces left and all sorrows are new.
It hurts, oh how it hurts, the ache within,
When love turns to pain and the heart gives
in.

When do we leave? When is the right time?
Is it when love fades or when heartbeats
align?
What is right or What at all is time?
Just a mere phase as if life is just fine.

Why, and why do you want to stay?

Why be pretentious,
And with whom you want to sway.
You are tired, you pray and pray,
When will it be the sunshine, and when hay?

But still, we hold on to the love we once
knew,
A glimmer of hope in a heart turned blue.
Perhaps, someday I will be the one sunkissed,
Forgiven and forgotten, and nothing will be
missed.

12. Pause

Pause

The sunset beckons and day grows old,
Birds return to nests and feathers fold,
People pacing with their footsteps fast,
Racing home as the world slows at last.

And you, my love, you awaken anew,
To a world within waiting just for you.
Your journey familiar yet unknown to sight,
Your path unwinding through pauses in
flight.

You've travelled far and think you've grown
wise,
But pause dear traveller and sit to realise,
There's a new piece of you is yet to be told,
A hidden chapter that's still waiting to
unfold.

Discover this piece and own it as your own,
A fresh awakening to a world of the
unknown.
In the stillness where shadows pause and play,
Lies a new beginning at the end of each day.

So wake up dear and take the road less worn,
And find the new you that's been waiting to
be born.
In the pause lies your chance to renew,
To discover the world, that's waiting for you.

13. Love All

Love all

What is this sound that I hear,
On the table-land, farthest but not near,
I trek and trek while I push the fear,
Little whispers as dawn gets clear.

With each step along the hillside,
The table-land stretches far and wide,
A natural canvas where the wonders reside,
Nothing stops me, as there is nothing to hide.

Right at the top, I found my little spot,
Humbled amidst the mountain top,
Peak at its vast had got me caught,
As I closed my eyes to see the picture shot.

The valley of the Krishna river, down it lay,
This sky of sombre green below me sway,
The serene, the truth, the love, I may say,
Created memory and more belonging as I
stay.

Nothing hidden, all revealed as I stand tall,
Am I yet to live after my many deaths small,
No desires, no secrets, just the divine call,
Enveloped with harmony and love for all.

14. Close your Eyes

Close your Eyes

Sit upright and focus your gaze within,
Between your eyebrows, let love begin.
Behold the darkness as joy fills your heart,
Watch as love and only love as your part.

A tiny spark and a light in the wonder night,
If you focus, it expands and grows a wondrous sight.
Enveloping your body with a radiant glow,
Filling your home and all that you know.

Neighbourhood, city, state and nation too,
Bathed in joy with love shining through.
Asia, Europe, America and the sane world,
Drenched in light like a precious pearl.

The Earth, a tiny ball floating free,
In a sea of joy, the wild and carefree.
Planets and stars like diamonds, all bright,
Glittering in the light, a blissful celestial
sight.

Expand this love and let it grow and thrive,
Realise this joy that's always and ever alive.
No boundaries, no limits, just the feeling of
one,
Inside you, the world floats like the morning
sun.

Open your eyes, look at your body small,
Close them again and remember it all.
You're not your body; you're the space within,
A beauty full of harmony and love begins.

15. She is the Journey

She is the Journey
Waters quite harsh and meadows not green,

Alone, she was crossing the rivers unseen.

Rough were the days but she was sunkissed,

Life has its ways, but nothing was missed.

Jerking and shaking but she was flowing free,

Thrusting but trusting what eyes can never see.

Let her flow with all the force while creating new paths,

She is bound to grow, and she knows in spite of fleeting wraths.

She will not stop now, till she meets the sky,

Lightning, thunder, hail, whatever comes by.

She is now on her journey, the journey she is,

He is always waiting, waiting for who she is.

One last lap of his orchestra he plays,

She goes dancing for His soul she craves.

16. Two Feet

Two feet

Suddenly, two feet came close to mine
In the night, amidst heavy rain's shine.

The street was aglow, a wondrous sight
Closer, he held the umbrella tight.

Suddenly, chaos faded to fine,
As I looked up into his soothing eyes, that shine.

My gaze met his and my heart melted fine,
His tall, lean body, so close to mine.

I felt the warmth spread down my spine,
He stood there, looking at me in mime.

His feet so close and my heart's flatline,
Oh, I lost everything that was mine.

That moment stood still and was slow,
The world around blurred, though ready to
glow.

The raindrops sparkled like stars so bright,
The heartbeat lost its rhythm in my body
tight.

As his lips took a curve to its side,
Mine trembled, and the soul took flight.

17. Temporary Permanent

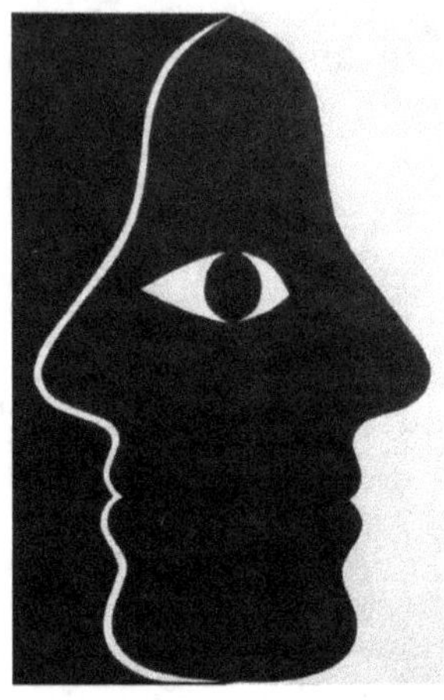

Temporary Permanent

I had a hard time walking past one,
Looking and admiring, noticing none.

My gaze was not a temporary one,
It was a permanent fleet that had begun.

Time's dance and my swaying free,
Rolling clocks and my longing spree.

Was it the February chill or October's glee,
Treasuring memories that cease to be.

Moments are temporary, lost in time,
Memories permanent, forever mine.

Dry tears and unknown fears are fine,
But Your stone glare tears me to pieces,
divine.

18. The 51ˢᵗ Street

The 51st street

Billboards and skyscrapers, a towering sight,
The bold dance of neon lights, a starry night.

The palette with colours, an artist's delight,
Was I a captive or the freedom in sight.

The street held high while all sets go by,
A few fast and clear, while some sheer and
shy.

Some were rushing down to the subway,
While others in the crowd paving their way.

My gaze slipped down onto his feet,
So close to me on 51st Street.

19. 45th Year

The 45th year

The pain was so rare and deeply real,
Beats grappling with unbearable fear,
Haunting my thoughts from ones so dear,
No trust, no love and only a flaming flare.

Unbearable was the thought of being hated,
All my love doings were finely grated,
Why was I not comfortable with the hatred
I've known,
Is it because it was from, so dear of my own.

Why do I think I need love to belong,
Am I not enough to love myself that I always
long.

Very late, I realise that there is no right and
no wrong.
Time tests, what stays and what comes along.
Everything and everyone has a life, a song,
You, me or maybe a bond so strong.

Everything, everyone and all relations die,
Whether it's brand new or aged, all say
goodbye.

20. YOU and me

YOU and me

Only if I let my mind swing and sway,
In your very thoughts of happy and gay,
I can save my life from stale and stray,
Please be by my side at all times I pray.

In this mystic world, full of beauty and crude,
Give me the courage that I open only grace
fruit,
Choice that I always have to be is civil or
rude,
Give me the art to catch my mind and heart,
all nude.

Love can either destroy me or empower,
Anger can either guide me or overpower,
Question is whether I am willing to own or
hire,
All I need is your touch and a belly full of
fire.

21. Home

Home

What is Home?
Is it the space that makes me whole?
Or where my heart finds its peaceful role?

Is it the boundary that keeps me in line,
Or the four walls that shelter the heart and
mind?

Is Home where belongings gather and stay,
Or people who love me, come what may?

Is being together a sense of Home?
Or is it when my heart is no longer alone.

When footsteps steady and love shines bright,
My face smiles, and my heart feels light.

Joyful tears fall like the morning dew,
Longing fades, and my soul feels anew.

When I'm just me, with no space for pretence,
Even sad endings can't dispel the essence.

At all times and all times, it's true,
Home is where love resides, and my heart is
renewed.

22. One Call Please

One Call Please

Dominating, enforcing, intruding,
He was everything but a friend.

Not me; he starts my morning
Calling me daily without failing

Not letting me be me and be my own
He calls me at dawn and doesn't leave me
alone.

To wake me up, to force me to rise
At morning tea time and me to exercise.

He advises me what to do and what not,
As now I am in marriage and all caught.

Staying miles away and distance couldn't stop
Not a single day when he had missed his call.

Irritated and angry but couldn't say a word,
He forcing and suppressing and I wasn't
heard.

Also, at times, I grew into a rebel
Will do everything but what he spells

Years passed by and he didn't stop,
He pursued calling me at all cost

Every single morning his call came at 4:30
As though it was his first day, even at 70

I am sure he got my unsaid loud word
Nothing stopped him, and he let go unheard.

I am big and have girls to nurture now,
Can you please stop and allow me to know
how.

Life is conquered when you wake up at dawn,
he said,
He would start before the sun's journey tread.

He can go to any length and has no
inhibition,
As helping all and helping friends was his
only mission.

Whenever I arrived from Mumbai to see,
The city that flaunts, so dear and just be.

He waited at the main gate of the house for
me,
The printed scarf around the neck would be.

Rubbing his cold hands, his head covered
I see his faded glimpse amidst the fog geared

Why doesn't he have the patience to wait
inside,
All he knew was force and dominance, I cried.

Leave me be alone and don't teach me,
I have my life, and let me build me.

The day came in January cold
He finally moved on to build new and bold.

Has he forgotten to wear his favourite scarf,
Isn't he feeling cold on the brick of ice, I ask.

Why is the gate full of people but you,
I entered with an empty glimpse of you.

Today, in my balcony,
As I sip my hot tea from the blue kettle,
And look down on my phone and settle.

Why It doesn't ring anymore,
Mornings have something that's missing at
core.

All gates are empty and no one's waiting,
Is he inside and am looking out creating.

One call, only one call *na*,
Now I know it was your love and only love,
Pa.

23. Truth or Dare – A Toast to Courage

'Truth or Dare – A toast to courage'

Truth or Dare, the play grind,
A toast to courage, heart and mind.

I choose truth and secrets will unfold,
Revealing me, my young and old.

A whispered confession pure to ears,
A soul laid bare in many many years.

Or if I dare, my actions will ensue,
A bold deed to test courage anew.

A leap of faith or a step unknown,
A heart that beats in a danger zone.

The choice to be made, the risk to deal,
To bare my soul or dare to feel.

Will truth set me free or dare ignite,
A spark within this grateful sight?

The dice are cast and the game begins,
A journey through my courage wins.

Truth or Dare, a war in play,
To face myself and fear to display.

For in the end, it's not the game,
But to own the space and no blame, shame.

My truth, my dare, my heart's desire,
Is it a reflection of my inner fire?

The whispers of my heart and fears I hide,
The doubts that creep and gear its stride.

But life's Truth or Dare doesn't always ask,
It demands, it pushes, it shapes and tasks.

To confront the fears and face the lies,
To choose the dare in lows and highs.

In each moment there is a test,
To bear the truth or dare to quest.

To find my voice, to stand my ground,
To sew my story with every truth profound.

24. Dance

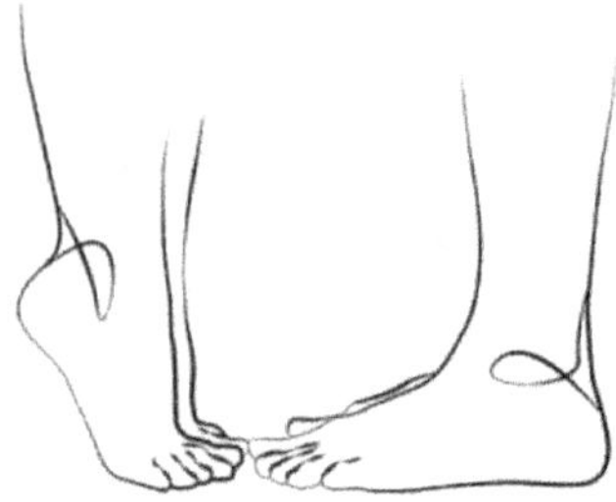

Dance

Lights are dim and candles are lit
Music is on as we take a twist
Your soft hand on my curvy waist
And the other cradles the wine to taste

Swirling me and holding me tight
Music whispers loudly the dark of night
Your hand in mine, a gentle guide
My heart beats slow where love resides

On the floor, dancing with you
Gazing into your eyes, my heart's anew
In the soft glow of fading light,
Our love grows to an endless night.

The moon and stars are witnessing us one,
In this sweet little dance, we have just begun.

25. Embracing Flaws

Embracing flaws

When I was 10, my life was cool,
Until that day in my school,
My partner stuttered and I tried,
To understand, to step inside.

Mirroring her words, I felt the pain,
Suddenly my own voice stuttered in vain.

I withdrew into my own shell of doubt,
Laughter echoed, tears fell, my voice routed
out.

Class oral tests, a fearful sight,
I refused to speak, hid from the light.
My art and painting, my words on page,
Became my solace and my hidden stage.

They thought me shy and I was blessed,
No assertive voice, no fights, no stress.
I smiled to appease, to fit in,
But I lost myself with each careful step
within.

Harsh self-judgment, unworthy and defective,
I compensated with style and smiles
protective.
Quietly following others were safe and saved
Drifting me away, although my voice craved.

I played hide and seek, a game of disguise,
Erasing myself with tear-stained eyes.
Nobody ever found me, hidden I stood,
A stranger to self or somebody unknown in
this hood.

But was silence the key?
Voicing truth shall set me free.
I broke the chains, spoke my heart,
Embracing flaws, a beautiful new start.

26. My First Crush

My first crush

When colours filled the air,
Happy painted people in joy so rare,
Magenta, red, yellow and blue,
All floors too painted in abstract and hue.

All were busy painting each other in spree
Water balloons splashing and colours flying
free,
Laughter, fun and music all delight,
Celebrating life with friends and all wild.

Being my all-time festival favourite
Jalebis, bhujias and sweet *samosas* we ate,
Taste buds dancing and asking for more,
As the colour revealed secrets and roars.

Suddenly a face with colour magenta
Appears in front of me holding a Fanta
In no time he emptied the bottle over my
head
And quickly, with a handful, coloured me red.

Well was it the colour on my face,
Or he helped me mask the blush on my face,
Always pretend to fight yet secretly thrilled,
Waiting to see him, my heart's never fulfilled.

But little did you know amidst the hue
My heart beat faster thinking of you,
A secret crush locked deep inside,
Unspoken feelings my heart did hide.

In the chaos of colours, I search for magenta,
A glimpse of him or a splash of Fanta,
Years go by and memories smile,
For the colours of love that lingered for a
while.

27. Brother

Brother

A brother so distant,
A heart so cold,
A silence between us,
A story untold.

We once shared laughter,
Tears and memories too,
But now only echoes,
Of a bond that's true.

In your eyes,
A stranger's gaze I meet,
A familiar face,
But a heart that beats.

The warmth that we once shared,
Now lost in time,
Leaves me with longing,
And a heart that's aligned.

I reach out to you,
Across the empty space,
Hoping to reconnect,
And find a warmer place.

But like autumn leaves,
Our bond withers away,
And I'm left to wonder,
If we'll ever find our way.

Still I hold,
On the memories of our past,
here love and Laughter,
Forever seemed to last.

And though you may be distant,
And cold as stone,
In my heart, the brother's love,
Will forever be sown.

28. Unwritten Stories

Unwritten stories

In this book, awaiting to be unrolled,
Lie unwritten chapters, stories untold,
A blank primed canvas stretched high,
I let my words flow in laughter and cry.

I ink my words in a row, dancing on a page
The screen confines my flow in a cage
On page, words fall, crawl, yet ready to
scribble,
Where touch and feel reveal no riddle.

I turn the page, begin anew,
Leaving my past with all its hue,
Embracing the unknown, I create,
Writing my story with thoughts, initiate.

I continue to write, keeping it tight,
Amidst doubts and self-worth fights,
Did I crave for people's approval?
When each book of life is uniquely unusual.

I am the one to create and I follow,
It's my own and no need to borrow,
It's one little step that I want to tread,
Painting each word and day, pink or red.

The book is my own from the start,
I am the creator and I follow my heart,
I would love to love and live fully, rather,
As for the book of my life, I am the author.

29. Silent Screams

Silent Screams

In the depths of her soul, a silent cry echoes,
A soundless scream, a heartfelt plea,
Trapped behind masks, they conceal their
pain,
Afraid to speak, fearing to be judged again.

The weight of the world, a crushing load,
Her little fragile mind still struggling to cope,
The silence is deafening her, a heavy rain,
Binding her voice and suppressing her pain.

Yet in the darkness, her spark remains,
A glimmer of hope, her light sustains,
A whispered promise like a gentle breeze,
If only she knows, a force to reckon, she is.

30. Rewinding

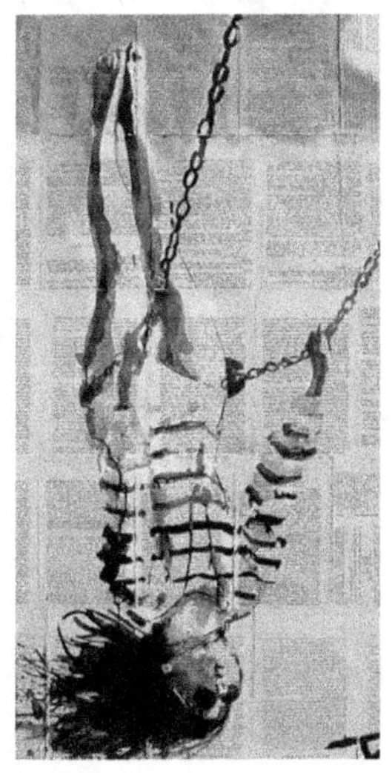

Rewinding

I wonder,
Did I leave smiles on the face or
I just cared for people already in the grave,

When I left,
Did I leave the place better than it was or
I left them to clean the mess caused.

Did someone long to meet me again or
They wish they never saw me and refrain.

Did I touch the people who I met or
Left them, that they just existed as I said.

Did I earn my day today as I sleep,
Or loaded my tomorrow with all the things I
keep.

Did I smile and hugged a friend,
Or was I nasty in arrogance at the end.

Did I make enough use of the life I have,
Or let me sink in the fears and doubts I have.

I am rewinding and rewinding as I gaze,
Filling my learner's heart as I praise.

Living each moment as it defines,
Well, we all are acting and it's fine.

Why be confined to what we were known,
Rewind is to learn and redefine your own.